T0190586

DEAR DARKNESS

DEAR DARKNESS

POEMS

Kevin Young

Alfred A. Knopf   New York   2018

THIS IS A BORZOI BOOK
PUBLISHED BY ALFRED A. KNOPF

All rights reserved. Published in the United States by Alfred A.
Knopf, a division of Penguin Random House LLC, New York,
and in Canada by Random House of Canada, a division of
Penguin Random House Canada Ltd., Toronto.

www.aaknopf.com

Knopf, Borzoi Books, and the colophon are registered
trademarks of Penguin Random House LLC.

Library of Congress Cataloging-in-Publication Data
Young, Kevin.
Dear darkness : poems / by Kevin Young. — 1st ed.
p.   cm.
ISBN 978-0-307-26442-8
I. Title.
PS3575.0798D43 2008
811'.54—dc22   2008007957

Manufactured in the United States of America

for my father
Paul E. Young
"BRUDDA"
1942–2004

and my grandmother
Joyce Pitre Young
"MUDDA"
1921–2004

Everytime you see me crying,
that's my trainfare home

—Traditional gospel moan

Contents

BLACK CAT BLUES

SAY WHEN

GREAT WEST CASUALTY

*

NOT TODAY

DEAR DARKNESS

Watching the Good Trains Go By

Only the stones
know my name.

The back of our family's
        King James
forgot my birthday

but still keeps a blank space
for my death date.

Sleep a strong wind
that once let me drift—

now, airless nights
        strand me
in my battered boat.

Fiddle without a bow.
Pawnshop guitar.

My mouth a harp,
heart a harmonica

in coat pockets so thin
        the wind
is my accompanist.

Sleep, I sing.
Forget weeping.

Watching the good trains
        go by—Washington
& Dominion, Santa Fe—

I think of jumping a boxcar
wherever stays cooler

than this here dirt
     red
as a wound, or the bottom

of the pot boiling
     the cure—red
as a child's backside

whupped till he cries
     & then's switched
silent again.

A torn tom-tom.
Banjo without strings.

Keep me, I sing.
Forgive leaving.

Only the stones
call me home.

SWEET BLOOD

Sweet Blood

Like stars the mosquitoes
swarm. He's gone. We sit

unscreened on the porch,
my father doused

in bugspray, that sweet-sick
stank. We drink

because my father's father he buried,
because the road will not carry

anyone but cousins, or neighbors
whose silhouettes and dust

we know. We drink.
Only son of an only son,

I do not share
my father's sweet blood—

what draws the skeeters
near him, braving the repellent

cloud, his quick hands, for a taste.
Finally my father gives—

I'm getting eaten up—
and heads inside

slapping red his legs.
Somewhere by the highwayside

my grandfather rests, his body
vaulted in ground that does not shift

we hope, or give back its dead.
We drink and forgive

the bugs who come for us
with dusk, who draw blood

the way we swallow
thin beer and words

like *love*—in order
to survive.

Cousins

This is for Tonia who learned to ride
a boy's bike at four, filling its basket
with a Chihuahua smart enough to open
doors—this is for Angela who taught me
to kiss but denies even remembering it—
for Big Red, born the color of Louisiana
dust, the rusty dirt we blew up
come Christmas when fireworks stands
slanted like makeshift roadside mangers.

This is for two sides of one family,
two towns full of folks I'm related to
or soon will be, summers finding girls
cute till someone says *That's your cousin,
boy,* then not looking again—this is for
all those names, Kiris & Makarios,
Omar & Cheryl, even for Jarvis
who broke toys I was too old to own,
then asked *Who broke dat car?*

to throw me off his trail. For Nikki
who cried whenever I did, sad
for the world's aches, mine, who worried
aloud in the movie that Indiana
Jones would *get deaded* till I explained
he can't, he's the hero. This is for Keith
in that unsunned room he hanged

himself like the paintings he masterpieced
& my grandmother's wood-paneled
walls still keep up—for his little sister Jamie
pigtailed & crying at his grave, begging
her brother back—Jamie who once refused
to sit by me, the older cousin never seen
before—Jamie who wouldn't eat

crawfish until I peeled some & she warmed
& laughed & ate & informed a roomful of family
Kevin's my cousin—yes Jamie, I am yours
& Phyllis's & her baby Brittany's
who ain't a baby no more, just a womanish
four-year-old going on forty— I am cousin
to her little brother who carries Keith's name,
carries this word, *cousin,* that once

rested on our tongues before the story of ships,
before words new as worlds, tribes
turned to regret—you can hear it—the steady hum
of *cuz,* say it till it buzzes the blood, gathers
like the wasps who kept returning, pressing
against screens in my grandmother's gaping house
no matter how often we let them out.

Nineteen Seventy-Five

Since there was no better color
or name, we called the dog
Blackie, insurance no one would forget
the obvious. One of the few dark ones
in the bunch, the only male,
he died twelve human years later
standing on a vet's table—
when the news came Mama
Annie, visiting, gathered us
in a circle of hands, called up
Jesus to the touch, to protect.

But that year when beautiful
still meant Black, when I carried
home my first dog full of whimpers
& sudden dukey, we warmed him
in our basement with a bottle disguised
as his mother, we let his hair grow long
around his feet, just as ours did

around ears, unbent necks. Back
in the day, my mother cut my afro
every few months, bathroom layered
with headlines proclaiming the world's end,
our revolution. I cannot recall
when I first stepped into the reclining
thrones of the barbershop
when I first demanded to go there alone,
motherless, past the spinning white
& red sign left over from days of giving
blood, to ask for my head turned
clean, shorn, for the cold to hold.

I only remember how back then the room
seemed to fill with darkness as she trimmed
my globe of hair, curls falling like an earth
I never thought would be anywhere
but at my feet, how the scissors twanged

by these ears like the raised voice
of a Southern gentleman the moment after
some beautiful boy segregates coffee, no cream,
black, onto his creased & bleached lap.

Prescription

I am sudden as a city
fire. Halfway to nine, I am
somethin else. Burn baby
burn. City of Wind, City
of Old Lady O'Leary's lantern
left on. I eat TV. I sit close enough

to the screen my teeth change
channels. No one saw
it was the only way
I could see, without glasses
Big Bird blurred—
a bruise, yellowing. Not yet

an eye doctor, only
an intern, my father never
suggested spectacles
& emergencies woke
our house at three. To me
a father just meant beer

& beards, without either
his mouth looked the same
bare of his Lieutenant snapshot:
half-smiling; shaved; pale enough
the loud-talking Private
nigger hater didn't realize
his superior's color. I thought
all dads were built sturdy & too tired

to play; that girls simply
had to chase boys across
playground pave, playing
kissy-face, the fastest of us
gangling up monkey bars & aping
smooches back down at the mob.

Only Roxanne ever
caught & called me
boyfriend, even phoned
me up for a five-year-old
date—ice cream, parent escort.
Kindergarten the bullies
chased me too, wanting me
dead as men the mayor

registered to vote, though
I must admit I loved half-leading
thugs on, teasing their toadies,
yanking those pigtails who paid
protection being pretty. At Anaconda
Montessori I had all
I needed: books; lips bloody

& burning like the Tabasco Dad
dumped on everything; shins scraped
clean as carrots. I even perched
on Mayor Daley's crooked knee, posing
with a blond girl for the hospital
paper: the perfect
picture, two cute kids
of physicians, two colors
coming together as if from cataracts

the fifth floor treated Stepin
Fetchit for, Dad looking behind
them unbugged eyes. What did I care
if a woman beautiful & half
Fetchit's age saw something
in him, helped him check out? Still
green, a munchkin, I wanted only

to fashion the Tin Man when
we played Wizard of Oz, sought
a heart to fit my bullet-proof
chest. Instead, I'd end
up Scarecrow trying
to follow that high-yellow
road—first half-heartedly

then mindful of not landing
on cement hard as some sunken
gangster's shoes. Practicing
songs & falls over
& over, I learned to fear
fire, to weave & wobble but never
quite stumble the whole Jim
Crow way down—never bruise

blue as light from our
television, the Zenith
a giant, glassy eye
that kept me company, quiet
& not quite warm.

Tuff Buddies

for Robert Scott

No sign or behind warming
could keep us from careening
down hills or popping wheelies;
the blue brake on our Big
Wheels only helped us peel
out, skid. Robert & I were Tuff
Buddies, friends for life, two kids
thrown together like the sandbox
& swings our fathers put up
in the gap between buildings.
We dug & played but mostly
sailed down Buswell Street
on those glorified tricycles souped
up our own way, ripping off
hokey handle-ribbons that fanned
useless, bicentennial. We removed
the blue, low-backed safety
seat, then conveniently lost it—better
able to stand for jumps, dismounts,
we'd hit the raised ramp at hill's bottom
then leap & pray the same way Robert,
Superdog, & I once spilled out a red
wagon right before it swerved, then
plunged through the garage
of my new house. Beyond
that patched hole our hides paid for
my Big Wheel still rots. I wouldn't let
them sell it with the yard; I still love
the wheels' blue click, black scrape
of plastic tire on the walk. I guess
I'm still holding on some to days
like that, still counting ten

like when D Doc would come over, greet
Robert & me with a handshake, counting
out loud, clenching our fingers to what
we thought death. Whoever lasted
got a half-dollar & we somehow always

made it, miraculous. What did I know
then of love but licorice & the slow
Sunday smell of the drugstore
Doc built up himself, his wife GiGi's
church-long hugs? It was years before
I heard his real name or learned
he wasn't kin, more till someone
mentioned West Indian. Always
the gentleman, one of the first I loved
to die, his lean voice confessed that spring
the chemo was over—*Don't know
son, this stuff, it's got me by the bones.*
Mostly, I remember his hands large
numbing mine, numbering, at the end
sounding almost surprised—*My,*
he'd say, *you're quite the grown
fellow*—then his letting go.

Bloodlines

The roses, wild, along the road
grew white & red & wide—mud-
colored, meddlesome, they scratched
when kissed, like father's beard.

Little scarred us then. We heard
the rain stop & ran
out to smell the afternoon
after the fall—the high grass, damp,

left prints as if snow
anyone could track. We stuck
our faces among the roses, took
some as if breath—they felt wet

as a dog's nose, as nosy, bit
if you weren't careful. We
inhaled their scent like the cigarettes
my cousin had snuck—he asked

if I wanted to smoke—lit
two, drew. The storm burned
off & the skeetas came out
for blood, specially my cousin's

whose skin was sweet
as my daddy's. Only our menthol
kept them at bay. Lookout,
bird dog, I pointed

when I heard the adult's suspect
steps—we buried the butts in wet
earth but still got caught—
my grandmother sniffed us out,

hunting and hounding
the way only blood could.
She chewed us out like the tobacco
she spat at our feet, beside

the pale ends obvious as ostriches
or worms seeking air after storm.

The Halt-Cart

Out of the spot where once
the outhouse bloomed, out
from under tin roof, from slim shed
of grandfather clutter, of stray
metal & dogs, they wheel

the go-cart forth. Uncles pull
the cord of that chainsaw
on wheels, lawnmower motor
jerrybuilt to a seat—
it sputters, dying,

then starts. My father
goes first. Revs out
into the road, swerving
& swearing through dirt.
Stones kick up

like a chorus line.
I—only
son, hungry to eat
earth like Dad—am next.
Sit in front of Father,

fit just barely, bunched
by his belly pregnant
with beer. Mother warns us:
Careful. I steer & he gives her
gas—we buck & laugh

into the crawdad ditches
alongside the road. Stand
like water from last month's rain.
Mother's turn. She boards
the hybrid—half runaway

train, half bronco—& astronauts
for Texas, for the Gulf. Look
down the dust & she's just
a speck against cypress sky—
won't she turn back?

When she reins & comes round
again, it's too fast. Hits
the brake like a tree
but forgets to let go
the gas. The chain snaps.

She stops. Sunglasses shoot
off, scatter crows. Leaning
the fence that separates chickens
from bulls, the in-laws rib
Mom: *Should've nigger-rigged*

a plane stead of a stop-cart,
they laugh. Dad can't. He wanted
to go again. We search the stones
& long grass flattened
by figs that grab the ground—

still can't find the shades
that spared mother
from sun—still can't find
the pearl-grey chain
that made the day run.

Primary

The No. 2 carried what carpool kids
never knew: my first dryish kiss;
a pocketknife's slow
unpucker; Halloween-costumed
mornings before fake blood
smeared & the eyepatch
went. Faded the strange sallow

of doll skin, the schoolbus rolled
on like a rubber, a snicker
thrown from the bad kids,
bigger, who sat in the way back
& never fit the mirror. Smallish,
José & I boarded early but stayed

                  swaying
toward the front, quiet
behind the camel hump
the front wheels made the floor.
Each bump a chance to try
& bounce through the roof
in that beast. Out of reach

of names & hurled peach
pits, José spoke of Ecuador,
his family's blue leaving.
Melon seeds spat past,
scenery. An older tongue
stuck out like the one José had
left behind.

          Only time
we turned round was when
a cool kid stood, cussed out
the driver who braked & swore
if he didn't shut up
she'd send him walking
to wherever hell he called home—

while the bus pulled from
the curb, I watched his red
sweater fade like the look
inside an eyelid long after
sun's stare. His response still
played in my brain—

            a refrain
of *Take This Job*
and Shove It—feeling
green that a kid could invite
trouble, defy

trouble, then leave trouble behind.
Trouble welcoming him home.
In homage I practiced raspberries
& the bird for weeks,
scripted killer comebacks

only my reflection heard. Stuck
together on that ride like hair
filled with gum, kids
kept rows every color
of the crayon box: unbroken,
still labeled, few strayed

                outside
given lines or braved
the bus's white, warning stripe
in front. Following grades to home
room, we drew Pilgrims & Goldilocks
by the numbers, waxing in hair

straight & narrow, same shade
as the craven-colored road
I'm writing this from, riding.

No Offense

If you wonder why
I'm not laughing, go ask
Brian, the sixth-grade cutup
the one with the most dirty jokes
who requested the tribal African song
Tina Singu each music class, black
vinyl spinning while Brian made
faces, knocked his knees together
like eggs. If you are curious about
me, just ask the boy who riddled
the whole playground or me
& my friends walking
home: *What do you get*
when you cross a black person

with a Smurf? I am sure today
he would answer you, would explain
now that he meant No offense just
like he did then above the crowd
of girls leaning close or the boys
trying to get his timing down,
just as after the punchline
he always said *You know I don't*
mean you. It's OK. And when
you see that boy whose last name
I don't seem to remember, be sure
to tell him that this here Smigger

could care less yet could never care
more, that my blue
& brown body is more
than willing to inform
him offense is one hostage
I have never taken.

Field Trip

    Not enough
was the lunch I brought
but I didn't trade, stuck
to my small fare. While

others passed peanut
butter & pickles, I ate
my soggy sandwiches,
the one with mustard

    first. No dessert.
The field held on
to its secrets, the words
we kids got sent here to find,

names of trees & birds, Latin,
scientific. We gathered
samples, stirred under rocks
to study the world pale & near-

    sighted as the black albino
able to enter Cotillion, to pass
the brown paper bag
test at the door but still get

talked about. To this day
my father won't wear
baggy pants or carry his
lunch in bags—both remind

    too much of teenage
times, of days Negroes
had to lug lunch to town,
chicken grease or hocks

seeping the paper, making
the bag a newborn's caul—
the veil that lets you see
ahead. After all, who knew

when you'd end up downtown,
walking past miles of WHITES
ONLY signs or the thin disguise
of Gentlemen's Clubs. No one

had to wink or hint what
Members Only meant. Just head
out, hungry, past the boulevard
toward the dock or boardwalk

or fields that chain
& label nothing except
food. Alone, devour cracklin
& drumstick till no meat

or marrow is left, just
bones & grease
& fossil enough to feed
a father's fire.

Flood

That week the only gods were clouds,
turning horses, then guns—
we watched the storm
from the porch, waiting—and boy
it rained, fell like Jericho,
its walls. Water broke

through the roof. All
our pails were full—we'd bailed
the bedroom twice. My father
watched the pond his cousin
almost drowned in fill up,
ooze past the pighouse, and creep

toward us like the snakes that began
swimming past like question
marks, the future. Why was
the Old Man so angry? *He just
reminding us of our place.*
We sat as my Aunt walked past

in mudboots to her waist,
dodging snakes—all that
poison floating by.
We knew the levee wouldn't hold
because the Sheriff said
it would. This far from town,

only dry land was what white
folks owned; down here
no ark or anchor could save
us, or what was left
of Da Da's makeshift barn—
the roosters and pigs cooped up

together, the horses that just
stood and took it. In the end the flood
came slow, steady as a lover
or her ghost, a solid wind knocking
the pighouse down. Far fence posts
now islands. Our house bottomless—

whatever was under there
gone, or given up on—
then, gettin-up morning, the waters
receded suddenly, a hairline,
a widow's peak—left
the yard littered with crops

and change—a doll whose face
unpainted itself, flocks of doves
dead—the clouds became mouths
again, or suns, and the snakes
slunk back to their favorite
holes, at home in our lawn's

graveyard of cars.

Aunties

There's a way a woman
          will not
relinquish

her pocketbook
          even pulled
onstage, or called up

to the pulpit—
          there's a way only
your Auntie can make it

taste right—
          rice & gravy
is a meal

if my late Great Aunt
          Toota makes it—
Aunts cook like

there's no tomorrow
          & they're right.
Too hot

is how my Aunt Tuddie
          peppers everything,
her name given

by my father, four, seeing
          her smiling in her crib.
There's a barrel

full of rainwater
          beside the house
that my infant father will fall

into, trying to see
         himself—the bottom—
& there's his sister

Margie yanking him out
         by his hair grown long
as superstition. Never mind

the flyswatter they chase you
         round the house
& into the yard with

ready to whup the daylights
         out of you—
that's only a threat—

Aunties will fix you
         potato salad
& save

you some. Godmothers,
         godsends,
Aunts smoke like

it's going out of style—
         & it is—
make even gold

teeth look right, shining,
         saying *I'll be
John,* with a sigh. Make way

out of no way—
         keep the key
to the scale that weighed

the cotton, the cane
         we raised more
than our share of—

If not them, then who
      will win heaven?
holding tight

to their pocketbooks
      at the pearly gates
just in case.

Pallbearing

i.m. Mack Frederick Young
"Da Da"
1910–1992

LABYRINTH

Asleep beneath the house
he built himself,
the quilt sewn
from his worn-out shirts,

you wake to find Da Da
at the foot
of your bed, all angles
& thin—

his body
has become
an ankle, knotted,
skin barely

covering bone—
he clenches the posts
caught in moonlight
wanting to go

to the bathroom
by himself,
to refuse this return
to childhood, need

for someone else to help—
it is this he hates—
but tonight, trapped
in the blue maze

of his breath, he might
as well be a minotaur,
half man
half bull-headed spirit—

drawers grown
too big,
fallen around
his knob-knees,

he trembles, a leaf—
asks—in his mutter—
for his wife
of almost sixty years—

Get Mudda.
After she stumbles
him to the bathroom,
you want to ask

if she recalls
the courting, the slender
stones thrown
at her window—

so you do—
Go to bed baby
is all you get.
You can't. By morning,

much older,
you can see
soon he'll die like a day
does, slow

at first, then all
a sudden

like night, he'll fall—

PALLBEARING

In the end it all

comes to this—
wigs & rosaries
folks bent to knees

first time in years
God blond above
the casket

& no one singing
or saying a thing—
men holding

their hats, uncut hair
keeping porkpie shapes
some with smiles

& kisses for widows—
the clumsy crosses
hands old or amnesiac

make—folks laying
hands on the body
as if to heal—this

goodbye is gone
& we line up
to lift, a grand-

son's duty, bearing
the pall, like Paul
—my father's name

though few call him that—
following the hearse
lights low cross

water knee deep
in the road, a sea
no Moses can part—

rain no Noah's
seen for years—
I'm a get them niggahs

my Auntie says Da Da
dead, must have said,
making sure

there wouldn't be
too much drinking
& carrying on

over him. Da Da,
along the road
from the wake

to the grave, that black
dog could be you
sniffing at sugar cane

fallen from trucks—
a struck possum
on the shoulder—

At the burial site your weight
is mine—I toss white
gloves in the grave

before it's filled
& the saints go
marching past—

On the way back
to the house & the repast
& whatever else awaits

I still
bear you, lift you up
over fields, over cypress

& song The Kingpins
Baby
It'll Be Alright

from the radio
next to distant cousins
barbequeing for us

Brudda—my father—
sees the dark circling
looks up & says Never

seen this many
crows in all
my days—

VICTUALS

He is dead so we eat.
In his heaven he must be
hungry—so we fill
ourselves, stomachs,

for him—the red sauce
& the meat, acres
of pies Aunties have
blessed. In the yard kin-

folk I've never met
open the giant barrel grill
& smoke seeps out
the lid. He is dead. Bury

our faces in food
to forget, in vain, the rain
falling, fallen, water standing
like he never again.

HURRICANE

This must be after Audrey
blew in & tore the barn roof
off, my father says, pointing
out the picture—the old one

didn't slope like that. Da Da,
sure good at nigger-
rigging, had a new one up
in a week. You can't date

the photo from either face—
my grandfather baked
dark from the fields, my father's
baby fat holding up glasses

the only giveaway of age.
Must be fifty-two or three—
photo yanked from one of those
old Polaroids a cousin had,

edges wavy
as memory. Dad calls
the shoulder-high shotgun
slung across his elbow

all pose—Da Da, gun draped
over his arm, seems about
to say something,
or maybe the dog says it

for him, mouth slightly open,
panting—that's Shag,
Dad says, his brother
King had a longer nose

that's how you can tell.
Wasn't good
for hunting rabbit so Da Da
gave him away to a cousin,

made him a fine
deer dog. From the frame
I take the picture, slowly untape it
from sepia shots of kin

now only my grandmother
can name
or knows to claim—this little girl
that can't be her

but is. Though we buried
Da Da today
the yard hasn't changed—
see there, behind them

in the picture, still
unmended, the crooked brown

grin of the gap-toothed fence.

EULOGY

    All talk
is lucky. Just ask
my grandpere, growing
into earth, half-

French, all man-
drake screaming when pulled
from its roots. (You need
a dog to undo it properly, staying

just out of earshot.)
Below us he hears
as the dead must, the day
speaking to itself, muttering

as he did, going deaf—
from him sounds retreat
as if beneath great
water. The Gulf. The coin

on his tongue drug
him down. I do say—
I loved him. Lucky
to have told him. Our talk

black cats crossing
the path—rare
& dangerous. Don't give me
any lip. No jazz. Don't ask

me to say it any
better than this—our last
and only kiss, butterflies

fluttering shut like mouths
    above him.

See That My Grave
Is Kept Clean

Lost in the heat
we search the colored section
of the town cemetery

for my great-
grandfather's grave—
find only crumbling names

that sound French
& familiar, none
his. Deep weeds. Jesus

a statue facing just
the white stones—
crucified high above,

his back to us.

Insurance

Dependable as death, the white man
knocked each month, called
Mudda by her first name

& collected the next installment
for her burial. She paid
for her death fifty

times over, not just
in money, but if
you were there you'd see

that while he called her
Joycie
& she hunted for the money

she didn't have, had somehow
set aside, my grandmother shot
him a look

that if you knew
her, & only if,
was the oppposite

of affection—pity
perhaps, but more
like the disregard

the world had tried
tossing her way
& had failed. Even

his *Thanks kindly*
or *See you next month*
couldn't counter

her long stare after
he let the screen door
slam shut, rusty springs

tsk-tsking behind him.

Inheritance

The battered black box I brought
from my grandmother's house

held yellowed bills, receipts
for seed, chicken feed, and envelopes

full of promissory notes—
my inheritance held

in a box held together
by masking

tape, and more tape, browning
the metal, hinging it shut.

Everything hinged
on what bloomed inside

among the muggy smell
of old paper, and loans

long since forgiven—the seed
bought against earnings

in Sunset, the mill
NOT RESPONSIBLE

FOR UNATTENDED COTTON
LEFT IN THE YARD

ALREADY GINNED.
My grandfather's signature

few carbons held—
most bore the John

Hancock of some boss
I picture like death

or debt, looming—
misspelling Da Da's name.

Both, we hope,
are final—or is it only debt

that lives on
forever? I owe

them my life, my grandparents
who fought the elements

and the earth to raise me up,
and us, planted the seeds

of cotton, of promise
no box, nor coffin, can contain—

though this black,
broken, unlocked box, secured

and scarred by tape,
comes close.

Uncles (Blood)

Talk turns
to who has the sugar
& how much water
you should drink a day,
to conspiracy theories—*cornbread
can kill you*—

Uncles give advice
not gifts. They forget
your birthday but recall
how short you once were
forever. In your mind
they always loom taller

even years after bumping you
the Bar-Kays from an 8-track—
all bass & bucket seats
in the souped-up black Camaro
parked in the yard
they mean to mow.

Uncles will build half
a house, the frame, the place
the plumbing will go, all
beam & bone,
& never finish the walls

till one day the rain will
rot it all.
Uncles got plans
& they're big.
Uncles underestimate

everything but food, buy
in bulk then watch it
go bad. Uncles heal
with a touch & can fry
turkeys whole. Uncles smoke
menthols & speak

prophecy. Will lift
you above their head,
bad backs & all—will jerry-rig
a motor to an old-fashioned
lawnmower to slay

the weeds. Will lie
down after, exhausted,
prone on Mama's couch,
refusing to see

no doctor—dragged in
lucky, Doc'll say, hours before
shrapnel from some unseen
mowed-over tin
was about to bore

into their huge hearts.
Uncles lie
beautifully. Years later
Uncles won't much remember—
instead show you their watch

that's stopped—*It's ghetto,*
they'll laugh, flashing teeth
more gold than their timepiece
that's a copy
of a copy of a copy—
the battery run down

but still worn, still shiny.

Casting

I learned to shoot
that summer in Maine
my father studying
medicine & teaching
me what he called
survival. I sent BB's
or stones from a sling
through beer cans as
aluminum as the canoe
I figured out how
to row, each hole
an aim, exclamation.

Mornings, before seminars
on blindness & open
hearts, my father
taught me targets
& fishing: his unshaking
surgeon hands would thread
a hook, worm it, then cast out
like a leper, the pole
his unsteady crutch.
Gnats circled like verbs.
Dad paced that rotting

dock, threatening to cast
me in the lake—that'd
show me to swim all
right, and how.
That night I dreamt
the rental house
into water, woke
to wade among lures
leaned dark against
door frames, reeling
among what deep
I couldn't breathe.

Next morning, the trout
I yanked from the grey-green
lake stared back like the lung
it didn't have, mouth
opening & closed
in prayer, a dank flag
lifted feet free
of water I feared,
that damp even
my dog dared enter.

In the picture I look
happy as a trigger
holding the prize rainbow
high: dog, Dad, & me
glittering big as the fish,
rod & line stitching
us together like
the birthmark a doctor
removed so young
now only my slight,
side scar remembers.

BLACK CAT BLUES

Ode to My Scars

Soon I will be
              simply
that skin darkening—

   a flower burst
open, then
rouged, cut, lain

across the coffin.

      No nicks at first,
my hands now mostly

these scraps and seams—

skin which weeps like kin
when parting—

the way brown rivers
                  after baptism
ripple, kiss themselves closed.

Ode to My Feet

Crocodiles, eel,
spotted
dog and owl—
my feet flat

as a country mile.
They stand tall, talk

hardly, if at all.

My legs even manage
to reach down, meet

my low-lying feet!

And on rarest occasions only
does the right miss
the left, grown

wide and lonely.

Black Cat Blues

I showed up for jury duty—
turns out the one on trial was me.

Paid me for my time & still
I couldn't make bail.

Judge that showed up
was my ex-wife.

Now that was some
hard time.

She sentenced me
to remarry.

I chose firing squad instead.
Wouldn't you know it—

Plenty of volunteers
to take the first shot

But no one wanted to spring
for the bullets.

Governor commuted my term to life
in a cell more comfortable

Than this here skin
I been living in.

Childhood

Autumn & the leaves turn
to people—yellow, brown,
red—then die. Only ash
trees stay white, standing—

the woods welcome you, trail
like a tongue, half-hidden.
Ears cover fallen trees:
pale mushrooms, listening.

Stop & you can hear
the peckerwoods high up.
Where is nature
human? On the ground

bark thin & pale
as paper, coded Morse.
You are lost, path
unmarked. It grows

dark, you older, night
around you like a lake
you've swum out too far
into—tread moonlight

while the bugs begin
taking your blood
for their children. Wish
them well. Wave.

Adolescence

Gravity is screwed
up—nothing stays
when put down
like the class
outcast, or else

seems so heavy
it won't budge. Sit
in your room, not sent,
& wait for weightlessness

to overtake you.
Patience is almost
impossible. You've lost
something, something
dear, but won't look

for fear you'll find
what's missing. Wait
& like a nose it might
turn up. You hate

how your hands become
thumbs, your voice barking,
then breaking
a window. Wait.

Ode to My Sex

Like France,
it leans left.

Like that Tower
in Italy, its shadow
covers the city

though no one's dropped
stones from it
in some experiment.

In the wind
it bends, a suspension
bridge.

All night let's climb—
Manhattan, Bay, Golden Gate.

Blind Marxist,
it rises up valiant
and fails to understand

why even Russia
loves jeans blue.

(It's no pinko,
though.)

On occasion it's even
been known to don
a uniform
and salute!

Mercurious, it rises,
falls, a god
both liquid

and solid.

Short End Blues

I love you like barbeque
You leave nothing on the bone

I love you like barbeque
Leave me nothing but bone

You make me go hogwild honey
Make me want to hurry home

        *

Let's get dirty as chitlins mama
After we'll wash us clean

Let's get chitlin-fonky mama
Swear we'll wash up clean

(You know it may take two three times
of trying & rubbing & bleach)

I'll borrow our sweat & bottle it
to boil the sheets, to sleep

        *

Devour me like marrow
After kiss me quick

Go on & swallow my sweet marrow
Kiss me to the quick

When we love let's leave of each
other's bones only milk

Bachelorhood

Dream you are a moon
minus an earth, & here
you are: collecting sporks
& mustard from fast food joints

in case of company
that never comes. On your planet
the floor is grey—toilets
in their dirty orbits—

& footprints never fade.
You're Robinson stranded
on that island called yourself—
no Friday for you,

just this Sunday morning
feeling you are skipping church,
skimping on the tithes
in the collection plate. Your last meal

always yesterday. Phone
off the hook, pretending
busy—better that, than this silence
what won't quit ringing.

Lost Dog Blues

from Found #4

I was late to school
because I woke up late.

Please let me in.

Don't upset
the warden.

Clowns stalking
Clowns killing

Clowns cheering
Clowns stealing car.

Aging Hippies
Volleyball!

If it is left in the sink
look for it in the trash.

I don't know you but
I like you. Call me—

My number is 911.

The Word of Jesus
The Blood of Jesus

The Name of Jesus
Bomb for demons.

I have just as much
to loss as you.

Ask for Rusty.

Poison
Earthquake

Fire
Jenny.

Do you know about the frog.
Unfortunately I do.

Christ loves
even you.

Hang Dog Blues

I'm no angel
    But you're the manger
You're the town
    And I'm the stranger

I'm the beggar
    And you the cup
I'm an indoor umbrella
    You the bad luck

You're the vacation
    I'm the last resort
Me the kangaroo
    You the court

I'm a ghost town
    And you're the mayor
I'm a wreck
    You're Keller & Keller

I'm the leaf
    And you the blower
I'm the sod
    You the soldier

I'm the shoulda
    You're the coulda
You're the gravedigger
    I'm the widow

I'm what's left
    You're always right
You're the pugilist
    I'm a lightweight fight

I'm *Well You Needn't*
    You're *So What*
You the movie star
    Me the stunt

You're my Lil' Bit
    I'm the Big Flirt
I'm the desert
    You're just dessert

I'm the *Titanic*
    You're the rudder
You're the milkmaid
    And I'm the udder

Who's the statue
    And who's the pigeon?
Who's the ought to
    And who's just wishing?

I'm the lean-to
    You're gone fishing
You're the rescue
    I'm still missing

I'm the pie
    You're the piper
You're my baby
        Don't make me no diaper

To My Near-Mistress

Before he returned, your fiancé-
in-perpetuity
seemed taller, and tough,

though upon arrival stands
merely stocky,
his beard grown rough.

That night we held ourselves
and did not kiss
you were saving up for this?

The days you dressed
drunk in violet monochrome
seem to fly far, and fast

when you two walk past,
hands like flowers pressed—
a glance—you in mourning clothes.

Something Borrowed Blues

I finally found me
a nice girl

to marry—
I thought she'd been voted

Most Likely
& Pretty

turns out she
was voted Most Pity.

Went on down to the courthouse
& the test said

we were kin—
not blood

but same proof
of liquor stained our veins.

We eloped
anyway.

Her mama's name
was Backhand

& her daddy
called Jalopy—

they couldn't give her away.
She had her a voice

like an axe
& danced

like a pickup
wrecked beside the road.

We spent our honeymoon
at home

since hell was booked
till who knows.

Slow Drag Blues

I don't believe in sex

after marriage.
    My wife does, just

not with me.
    I plead the Fifth

of whisky. I am close

to perfecting a theory
    of forgettability.

Grief a dog
    that keeps dogging me—

Good Grief,
    I say. It's me

he's teaching to beg—

my next anniversary
    is newspaper, yesterday's—

lining my cage—
    Tomorrow the day

I hope to learn to stay.

On My Mind

I am tired of my
own mind. Its wanderlust
and lust lust, its mis-
trust of the blind
suck of sea—

With you all
is undertow.

With me the tide
is never enough—I become
beached, splayed
sandbound, dreaming water.

Flash Flood Blues

I'm the African American
sheep of the family.

I got my master's
degree in slavery.

Immigrant
to the American dream,

Evacuee,
I seen the water

Ladder its way
above me. Swam

To the savings & loan—
no one home.

I've steered
Hardship so long—

Even my wages of sin
been garnished.

Wolf tickets
half off.

Collect call
& response.

Whenever we pass
on the street

Death pretends
not to know me

Though the grapevine say
he's my daddy.

Lime Light Blues

I have been known
    to wear white shoes
beyond Labor Day.
    I can see through
doors & walls
    made of glass.
I'm in an anger
    encouragement class.
When I walk
    over the water
of parking lots
    car doors lock—
When I wander
    or enter the elevator
women snap
    their pocketbooks
shut, clutch
    their handbags close.
Plainclothes
    cops follow me in stores
asking me to holler
    if I need any help.
I can get a rise—
    am able to cause
patrolmen to stop
    & second look—
Any drugs in the trunk?
    Civilian teens
beg me for green,
    where to score
around here.
    When I dance,
which is often,
    the moon above me
wheels its disco lights—
    until there's a fight.
Crowds gather
    & wonder how

the spotlight sounds—
   like a body
being born, like the blare
   of car horns
as I cross
   the street unlooking,
slow. I know all
   a movie needs
is me
   shouting at the screen
from the balcony. From such
   heights I watch
the darkness gather.
   What pressure
my blood is under.

Bling Bling Blues

Once hunger
was my dance partner—

Now my diamond shoes
hurting my feet

& that my wallet won't
fit my 50s

are my chief complaints.

I'd like to thank
God, my agent.

My teeth went
platinum last week.

My ride's seats
golden fleece.

My greeting: Dog,
Black, Homey,
Money.

Once every stranger
was my father—

I went out & got my scars
insured.

I got more rocks
than the clink—

bought a gold-plated house
for my mama

& all my trophies.

Cheddar, green,
cabbage, cream.

My leaving:
Peace, a pound
of fist.

Once hunger——

Still, danger taps
me on the shoulder

wanting to cut in.

Set List

1. The Song called Sorry
2. Segue
3. The Song named Money
4. The Belly

5. The Slow One
6. Long tongue
7. What town are we in?
8. The Critic's Fave

9. Sneaking backstage
10. Maybe
11. The Quiet Chorus
12. Dark applause

13. Encore
14. Lights up, stomping more

Why I want my favorite band to break up

Reunion. Court
battle. Greatest
Hits Package.
Close call.

Possession trial.
Palimony. Alimony.
Best-selling
tell-all.

Obscure bootleg
worth more.
No last ditch
rehab record

with replaced lead singer
to endure.
Second
Farewell Tour.

Solo Projects.
Court Battle.
Underrated
offshoot band

by the rhythm guitarist
only I love.
The Early Stuff.
No more crowds.

No phoning
it in or selling out.
No slapdash
dwindling sales.

Christmas special.
Posthumous single.
Our long, never-final
farewell.

On Being Blind

Hard to compare pain—
So when the shortsighted
Pale girl lost her glasses

Whirling her hair
And arms on the dance floor
We all quit dancing

To look. From the stand the blind
Blues singer stopped to announce
Someone has lost their specs—

But she shouted back, *No, eyes!*
I've lost my eyes! Beneath his shades
The black and bluesman just smiled

And reached further
Into his monogrammed
Holster of harmonicas.

Dirty Deal Blues

Best advice I ever heard
I learned

at the poker table:
Shut up & deal.

I keep hoping for diamonds
or a handful of hearts

& getting only clubbed. Spades
to dig an early grave.

She said she was feeling flush;
turns out it was just a bluff.

I never call them
that raised me

since I split home.
My closest kin named

No One.
And him long gone.

Ode to My Father's Feet

No more fields.
No more walking
both ways, uphill, to school

And saying nothing until
now, when road is all

He remembers. Dirt. The old shoes
—*them brogans*—which I wear

He cannot bear—*We'd*
a cried if, when, we had
to wear those. His toes

Bare, bearlike, tufts
of dark hair in summer; his pale
undersoles that keep on

Softening, never will
—after standing so long—
turn full soft.

Up South Blues

Afraid there'll be
no cornbread in all the Midwest
     my Auntie
     arrives with a luggage heavy
with bursting boxes of Jiffy.

My father's cousin
keeps a potted cotton bloom
     in the corner of her brand-new
     flowered living room
to remember how far she's come.

My Auntie arrives
in Kansas with her luggage
     stuffed with Jiffy
     just in case
we don't have any.

My daddy's philosophy
always was
     We *shall*
     overcome—
& fresh ammo for my gun.

Ode to the Midwest

*The country I come from
Is called the Midwest*
—Bob Dylan

I want to be doused
in cheese

& fried. I want
to wander

the aisles, my heart's
supermarket stocked high

as cholesterol. I want to die
wearing a sweatsuit—

I want to live
forever in a Christmas sweater,

a teddy bear nursing
off the front. I want to write

a check in the express lane.
I want to scrape

my driveway clean

myself, early, before
anyone's awake—

that'll put em to shame—
I want to see what the sun

sees before it tells
the snow to go. I want to be

the only black person I know.

I want to throw
out my back & not

complain about it.
I wanta drive

two blocks. Why walk—

I want love, n stuff—

I want to cut
my sutures myself.

I want to jog
down to the river

& make it my bed—

I want to walk
its muddy banks

& make me a withdrawal.

I tried jumping in,
found it frozen—

I'll go home, I guess,
to my rooms where the moon

changes & shines
like television.

Ode to the South

I want to be soused,
doused

in gasoline
& fried,

fired up like a grill—

Let's   get   fired   up
We   are   fired   up

—I want to squeal
like a pig

or its skin. Gridiron.
Pork rind.

I want to be black
on the weekend—

I want God to root
for the home team.

I want to flood
my greens in vinegar

please.
I want everyone

to be named *man*.
Yes ma'am.

I want my cake
& to barbecue, too.

Propane, diesel,
rocket fuel—

It's not the heat it's
the hospitality.

I want to pray
on game day.

I want to sweat

in the shower,
to *shoot*

when I could say
somethin worse

like Jesus. I want a grill
of gold

& a God that tells

the truth, who sleeps
late on Sunday

& lets church out early
so I can make

the buffet.
I want the preacher to go late.

I want to give God
a nickname.

Uncles (Play)

There's a way a man walks
up to a counter, hands deep
in pockets, stands ten feet
away, waiting to order—*give me*

a minute—
There's a way a man will say
Let me have two
& doesn't mind everything costs

too much & will pay
for everyone even
though he can't afford it.
Why complain? There's a way

last names
ain't enough & first
don't fit, so family
friends, men, get

Uncle before them—
christened, like god-
sons, or ships, called
kin so long you forget

who's blood. Uncles ask
what you think
& mean it, eat up
all the yammer pie & get

forgiven. They believe
the world will end, will
tell you when
then laugh at themselves.

Play-uncles can show you how
to set up a stereo, drink
beer like water (that thin),
how to bet the horses

& how not to win.
Uncles know
how best to get to heaven
but give out

the country directions—
turn right by the old oak
catty-corner to the rock that looks
like a horse drinking its fill

& hang your first left
beyond the quiet hill.

YOUNG & SON'S
PAWN & GUN

Ode to Pork

I wouldn't be here
without you. Without you
I'd be umpteen
pounds lighter & a lot
less alive. You stuck
round my ribs even
when I treated you like a dog
dirty, I dare not eat.
I know you're the blues
because loving you
may kill me—but still you
rock me down slow
as hamhocks on the stove.
Anyway you come
fried, cued, burnt
to within one inch
of your life I love. Babe,
I revere your every
nickname—bacon, chitlin,
cracklin, sin.
Some call you murder,
shame's stepsister—
then dress you up
& declare you white
& healthy, but you always
come back, sauced, to me.
Adam himself gave up
a rib to see yours
piled pink beside him.
Your heaven is the only one
worth wanting—
you keep me all night
cursing your four-
letter name, the next
begging for you again.

Ode to Chicken

You are everything
to me. Frog legs,
rattlesnake, almost any
thing I put my mouth to
reminds me of you.
Folks always try
getting you to act
like you someone else—
nuggets, or tenders, fingers
you don't have—but even
your unmanicured feet
taste sweet. Too loud
in the yard, segregated
dark & light, you are
like a day self-contained—
your sunset skin puckers
like a kiss. Let others
put on airs—pigs graduate
to pork, bread
become toast, even beef
was once just bull
before it got them degrees—
but, even dead,
you keep your name
& head. You can make
anything of yourself,
you know—but prefer
to wake me early
in the cold, fix me breakfast
& dinner too, leave me
to fly for you.

Ode to Crawfish

Strange sailor, saint
of the roadside, cheap
date—for years you could be lured
into my arms with only
the promise of leftover meat,
a free meal. Dumb
but pretty, you give
me all I ask—all
I need do
is play you some zydeco,
buy you potatoes
& beer & water
& you're done for.
At the juke joint you curl
in my hands like hair
or stick out your tail
to warn me you're trouble.
Who else to trust
when you make it so easy
to believe everything could
be this good? Afterwards
you blush, embarrassed
by all the fuss. Some
think you need
to be gussied up,
taught French—but I know
your holy tongues
& for me that's enough.
Crawdaddy, craybaby,
your secret sweet keeps me
for hours, gets me
where I live—open up
& tell me everything
& I swear when I move on
to my next love, it's you
I'll still be thinking of.

Ode to the Buffalo

My daddy left you
cold, for me to find,
when he died. You mourn

him the only way
you know how—silent,
keeping me company, making

sure I eat.
For years it was you
we expected to go first,

had planned for every
eventuality, practically
picked out flowers. You ate

those years ago. Bearded
Lady of the Plains, your blue-
black tongue speaks

a silence I don't mind
& my father admired. You been
shot at a trillion times—

tossed like hoboes by trains
& survived. Bullshit's
Brother, you take guff

off no one, grow giant
yet fit, lean as a teenager
& as eager.

You're happy with a burger
& fries whenever
I take you out

but at a steak dinner
still know how to use silverware,
your touch both proper

& tender.

Ode to Wild Game

My daddy died loving
you, had since
he was eight. High school
sweetheart, long distance
romance, it's you he missed
most months
of the year, kept you near
like a picture, packed away
& pulled out when you weren't
around to remind him
he was alive. Out,
into the wild, the world,
is where you led. He died
hunting after you, you
are like pity—always
too much of you, or not near
enough. I miss
the way he held you
& like time would not waste you.
Elusive mistress
he'd later marry, you were
the midwife of his late happiness
& he was born at home
with no spoon in his mouth,
no hammer in his hand,
just his hard head
I inherited. At this hour
I bet you fear
you were better off
dead, you widow of the field,
you father gone too soon—
my grandmother of all mercy
who's outlived
her only, full-grown son
& never mentions the first
one who died
long ago young.

Ode to Homemade Wine

You are stronger
than you think. Quiet
cousin of mine, my uncle
made you & never knew
till years later
when you knocked at his door
& called him *father*.
Even his wife welcomes
you home. We all
seem loud with you around.
You fix the front porch
so it no longer leans—
take out the sting
the day my daddy's buried,
talking trash
& laughing. *You crazy,*
he would have said,
which where I come from
is a compliment. Mother
of moonshine, you swore
to get the jalopy in the lawn
running again, may get
around to it yet.
Though cloudy, you know
better than anyone
that death, while hell,
may make folks better—
you keep just
this side of rotten.
For you we've had to come up
with new names—
fermented, brewed,
settling in—but, lucky
for us, no funds.
Slow to anger, quick
to act, you are
the house my father
was born in, only last year

torn down to stop
from falling on this one—
the child's chair my grandfather
or his father made,
rocking, wood, painted
a green that won't
quit blooming
but must have seemed
to most folks only old, tossed
behind the house to rot
with the blackberries. Saved,
shipped, shaken
free of mites, that rocker
I found after my father's
funeral is like you—rickety
yet sturdy, you always
do the trick. You never
beg, nor borrow, save
all pain for tomorrow.

Ode to Okra

I like okry cause
it slips, said my old cousin
famously, & I agree—
all the more
filled with awe at all

you can do. Wayward
uncle, you grew up like a weed
yet were so much my age I called
you brother—like an eye
or early autumn you stay

red around the edges
& still green
at the same time. Tender
yet prickly, you gave gifts
whenever we needed them most—

visited each summer & lingered
much too long, mooching
your way through.
Though some nights I hated you
to us, & yourself, you were true—

stayed stewed,
never fried—the neighborhood
drunk, turned belligerent
& too tough
if ignored. Still

you weep when stirred,
make a gumbo worth
fasting for. Seventh son,
pilgrim, you once were a slave
I heard, a language

smuggled here in our hair
to teach us home
& what freedom
wasn't. In dusk
I've seen my father

cut you down—you, who
we prayed over each night
making sure, small
steady star, just for you
we saved plenty room.

Ode to Kitchen Grease

Once we were close.
Once we let you hold
our children, cook up
whatever you wanted—& cook
you sure could! You put your foot
in it, made food stick
to our ribs. Grey
grandfather, once clear
you grew cloudy
with age so we put you
in a home, & out
of ours. Little diva, bent
elder, you had grown
to be too much upkeep
& high pressure. Your nagging
sent many, favorite mother-
in-law, to an early grave.
Still, some mornings
you drop by, uncool, right after
breakfast bacon's been made—
sniffing round the kitchen
& already asking
What's for dinner—
& I sure wish you'd stay.

Ode to Grits

Like *y'all,* or sorrows,
or pigsfeet,
or God, your name
always holds multitudes—
is never just one—

unlike *moose* or *deer*
or death—which means both many
& alone. Little Lazarus,
you're the world before
the flood, & what's after,

are ash turning back
to a body. Done wrong,
you are the flavor
of a communion wafer.
Miss Hominy,

for years I misheard
your name as *Harmony*
& I was right. Kissing cousin
to Cream of Wheat, godmother
to oatmeal, no one

owns you, much less
no Quaker. Those mornings
over Strawberry Quik
when the kettle called
the Cream of Wheat cook

to meet me for breakfast,
you waited patiently to shine
the whites of your million eyes
on me. You must know
I love you by the way

I like you plain, maybe
buttered up a bit.
Salty, you keep me
on my toes, let me
believe, this once,

in purity—no cheese,
no grape jelly, no Missus
Butterworth's. Undoctored,
your cloudy stare
unlike my father's, his one

eye no bullet met
that, hours after he was shot
through the other,
I had to decide to give over
to someone still

alive, some girl or old
man whose vision—
even dead, ever
the healer—my father saved.
Resurrected like you

are daily. Welcome
stranger, pennywise
prophet, you are the wet nurse
of mercy, the rock
water makes speak.

Ode to Chitlins

i.m. Charlie Barfield
1950–2007

How do you like them wrankles?
asks my uncle, parish
constable, four
hundred pounds if he's
an ounce, & my best
answer may be: *A lot.*

Wrinkled wise man,
you are the kind of kin
I trust few hands
to help with—like his wife my Auntie
Faye's, whose name might
as well be Faith, for that's
what lets me let her

bring you to me
bleached, boiled, run
through the washing machine
till clean. Sweetbread's
sister, tripe's long
lost cousin, you're the uncle
I one day learnt

wasn't really—but I have grown
old enough, & young, to know blood
& family ain't always the same—
so you, I claim. You fed me
when I would have withered
without you, you weather me
like little else. I place

my hands upon you, old
family friend, & pray
you're well the way
my blood-uncle phoned
to pray with me after
my father died, when all
I wanted was his best

brisket, smoked slow.
Pork loin's poor brother,
you visit once a year, come
Christmas, if we're lucky—lately
even less. No use
waiting, or complaining—
your guts

are glory. Though your birth
certificate may read *Chitterlings,*
only Holy Ghosts' baptism record
gets your name right, like it did
my daddy's. Despite what
the newspapers say, your name
is not short

for anything, needs
no apostrophe. Those tight jeans
you wear, the ones with creases
ironed in—your linen
suit in winter—are out
of style & you don't care
who knows it. The road may seem long at first

you whisper, but see how brief
it's grown? The trail
may be full of shit
but you can make music
of even that. The last
place you'd look, you're hog
heaven—hard

to get to, much less
clean, you're where
we all end up. You are the finale
of most everything, grow
better with time
& Pace picante. Priest

of the pig, monk
of all meat, you warn me
with your vows
of poverty
that cleanliness is next
to impossible, that inside
anything can sing.

Ode to Greens

You are never what you seem.
Like barbeque, you tell me time
doesn't matter, that all
things wait. You take long
as it takes. Wife
to worry, you can sit
forever, stewing, grown
angrier by the hour.
Like ribs you are better
the day after, when all
is forgiven. Death's daughter,
you are often cross—bitter
as mustard, sweet
when collared—yet no one
can make you lose
all your cool, what strength
you started with. Mama's
boy, medicine woman,
you tell me things end
far from where
they begin, that forgiven
is not always forgotten.
One day the waters will part.
One day my heart will stop & still
you'll be here dark
green as heaven.

SAY WHEN

Lullaby

Sleep, shelter me.
Shuffle

me back into the deck
where I belong—

Sing no shout
your favorite song

until I fall
into your empty arms.

Let me be what
dust has to be, settling

over everything
& I promise to dream

of new houses & old
loves no longer. I swear,

sweet sleep,
I will summon no one

if you make me
again mine.

Sunday Drive

I been called by God
to testify
against him.

And the heart in its hole
knocks trying
to get out.

Pretty cage.

Sorrow the plate
scraped clean—
it's neither the food

eaten too fast
to enjoy, nor the empty
plate, but

the scraping.
What a song.

All night
long the silence
singing. The moles

making their way
beneath me while I sleep.

And Houdini, who could
escape anything, all
he wanted was to find

a way to speak
with his dead mother, so spent

most his life
proving séances false.

Now that's love.

He died
because he wasn't ready.

Me, I'm secondhand
like sections in the bookstore

I never noticed before—
Mysteries, or Used
Philosophy.

Downtown a hotel declares
Welcome
Great West Casualty.

Why not
decide the road along the rise
past the drive-in

showing nothing

& the church sign on the fritz
flashing like lightning.

Hard Headed Blues

Me & the Devil are rivals
for God's affection.

I can't say who wins.
My father's name

is Fate,
my son's Sin.

My guard dog's got laryngitis
& knows just one trick—

how to let folks in.

Came home early to find
my fiancée stolen—

her ring's gone to pawn
& my television's walked off—

Can't say I mind
that girl's gone

& that crackerjack ring wouldn't
cut anything

but why take my Zenith
with the good reception

& leave the one
with sound alone?

I tried but God's
still unlisted.

I don't mind using
love letters for fire

but at least leave me
some whisky

to fan it higher.

Order your air-
conditioned coffin today.

I'm sick of listening
to beauty

pageants, I can't say
who wins. They keep on

rescheduling Armageddon

but only seats I can get
are in the nosebleed section.

Even Heaven
has evictions.

By accident
my obit ran early

& only the taxman
& that damn dog showed

to mourn me,
his bark's mute trumpet

my only eulogy.

Stay

These days I walk with Death
around the block like a dog

only I'm the one begging
on my knees, barking

questions to the quiet.
Can't quit digging

for where your bones be

Another Autumn Elegy

I'm afraid God
is gone.
The wind yellowing

the trees, then baring
them brown.

The stars turned small

are all that's left
us. I've gotten word
God's up

& called it quits.
Who can blame em?

Or it—
whatever touches
us & says *this*

& *this,* takes away
& does not explain.

This is called faith.

This is the ground
grown hard, the mole
still managing

to push up parts
of the yard, piles of brown
dirt each night

the blind make more of
than I can,
or might.
        At night,
even the blind can see—

dreaming color, blues
or remembered green.

Tonight I'll wander outside
in the peacock dark

hoping to find
God like a man

in the jailhouse,
twenty to life—

planning escape the while—

I'll dig up what swallows
our brown hands

& for once not ask why.

Burial

i.m. Darrell Burton
1960–2002

It's time for the tulips
to be placed
gently in the ground

their thick heads resurrecting
in spring.

Quick, before the cold.

Too late—
the white wanders
tonight over everything & stays

despite the sun.

They say the smoke
is what got to you—

It is never the fire.
Next time,

I'll tell you sooner
that your blues
were beautiful, and your own,

but I still cannot say
they'll ever go away.

Toll

Damn bells—
on the hour

ringing, remind
you're not here.

Wonder will
they ever end?

The answer sends
a laugh like a breeze

between
the winter trees.

Death Letter

I got a letter this morning
How do
You reckon it read?
    —Son House

Say *slaughter.*
Say *father.*

Say the thing that
means nothing.

Say the thing.

Say the numbers
of the names

of the dead.
The lost.

Say there's
a difference.

Say *distance*
& *down* & *between.*

Say the names.
Say *shame*

& mean forgetting,
say *forgetting*

& mean never.
Say river.

Say the thing
not the name

of the thing. Say
they are the same.

Save me.

Daylight Savings

Like money the light
doesn't go

as far these days

Say When

Some days there is nothing
of the blues
                    I can use
so I put down
my pen & walk instead

humming *Memories
of You* by Louie
Armstrong—
                    it won't be long
before I have forgotten

the words, & soon
enough the words

will have gone
& forgotten me—

the silence we all meet.

I guess at God—

        the road twisting east
or south toward
the quarries,
                    fading light.

My body rejecting
my own heart.

Trees touching
above the buildings.

I want to raise
my face
to the blackboard sky—

forgetting how hard

it is for me
not to believe—

& scrawl my name
on a slate

no hand can erase.

Quartet

I am tired of this place & want to take
a slow train to the moon—

Just jump the rails out past the pale
peeling walls of this here room.

I feel like a dog that done lost his tail,
& keeps barking: *soon? so soon?*

Lay down outstretched among hail
& fallen stars, the rain's raggy tune.

Book Rate

It's getting harder
to live without

faith, or you,
or whatever

we choose to call
what calls

to us in the quiet.

The cat that sleeps
on my mailbox, yawning.

The sky dark
at noon & soon

snow salting the ground.

Days almost zero.

What this world is
isn't enough

& that's enough—
or must be.

Steady flurries.

I want to enter the earth
face first.

Hurry—

New England Ode

i.m. Richard Newman
d. 2003

Straight-backed pews
painted white
Compost, not trash
Boston marriage
Public school or Private
Paper, not plastic
Frappe, not milkshake
or malted
Rotary, not roundabout
Where do you summer?
Native, native, tourist
My loneliness
study group meets Thursdays
Shore, coast, overfished
Soda, not pop
Wetlands, not swamp
No Sunday Sales
Irish Twins
I'm a vegetarian
though I still love lamb
Pulpits high up
Spas, bubblers,
dry cleansers
Pineapple fences
Red tide
Sparkling or still
Woodchucks, not groundhogs
My dog & I
are both on a diet
Pay at the counter
Do you smell fire?
This is our year
All we need
is some good pitching
The Begonia Club
Volvo Volvo Volvo
Volvo Honda Volvo

The town my great-
grandfather founded
is just a tiny one
Fans, not a/c
Indian pudding
Patriot's Day, Bunker
Hill Day, Evacuation Day,
Lime Rickey
Curse, not pennant
Hiss, not boo
Pews you unlatch
to climb into, then lock
shut behind you

Amen

Belief in God is proof
people exist.

Ode to the Hotel
Near the Children's Hospital

Praise the restless beds
Praise the beds that do not adjust
    that won't lift the head to feed
    or lower for shots
    or blood
    or raise to watch the tinny TV
Praise the hotel TV that won't quit
    its murmur & holler
Praise visiting hours
Praise the room service
    that doesn't exist
    just the slow delivery to the front desk
    of cooling pizzas
    & brown bags leaky
    greasy & clear
Praise the vending machines
Praise the change
Praise the hot water
& the heat
    or the loud cool
    that helps the helpless sleep.

Praise the front desk
    who knows to wake
    Rm 120 when the hospital rings
Praise the silent phone
Praise the dark drawn
    by thick daytime curtains
    after long nights of waiting,
    awake.

Praise the waiting & then praise the nothing
    that's better than bad news
Praise the wakeup call
    at 6am
Praise the sleeping in

Praise the card hung on the door
　　like a whisper
　　lips pressed silent
Praise the stranger's hands
　　that change the sweat of sheets
Praise the checking out

Praise the going home
　　to beds unmade
　　for days
Beds that won't resurrect
　　or rise
that lie there like a child should
　　　　sleeping, tubeless

Praise this mess
　　that can be left

Redemption 5¢

Poor God, people everywhere
swearing to you all day

Ring of Fire

At the strip
club we come

for the ladies but stay
for the buffet.

In Vegas we feel paradoxical
as jumbo shrimp—

Everything here is for sale
& what's not

for sale is free.
In walks Dennis Rodman

hat pulled low, wearing a disguise
in hopes

of getting recognized. Between dances
they announce him

over a microphone
like bingo.

When we return
to our hotel, dawn

has long gone
& the pool slowly fills

with fools drained
like us.

We brown our already
brown bellies

& I ask my buddy
Think anyone

would guess us black
boys are a doctor

& a professor?
It's not that folks can't

imagine it, just
they don't even bother

to consider us
at all. Unlike us,

our drinks are expensive
& too strong. All night long

at the Hold'em table
we'll gamble it all

like tin men hoping
for hearts.

May Day Blues

I am Professor of Apologetics.

I am a person of interest.

This is not a test.

I am a prophet
    of the margins.

I demand a rematch.

I prefer my cars
    not so much used

as betrayed.

I am For the War but
    against the Troops.

I would waste six or so lives
    on you.

With you, I'd spend two
    of my three wives.

Out back my blues
    are buried.

I have nothing to declare.

I'm not here
    to make friends.

Mission Accomplished.

I demand a recount.

Reading *Animals Without
       Backbones,* 3rd ed.,

found out I'm the star.

Farm Team

I'm sick of this century
already.

My pleasant things all
ashes are.

No horizon—you can tell
the sky & ground

apart only
by guessing.

Rookie mistake.
Misery

is the only company
that would hire me

& I learnt yesterday
I'm getting laid off.

I wish wrong

& too often.
My pension

long gone, my job farmed
out to someone

better at failing—
I've been trained

in nothing.
I have taken myself

apart in the dark—
put back

together like a soldier
in the rain—one gear

always left over.

I shall be released

What we love
   will leave us

or is it
   we leave

what we love,
   I forget—

Today, belly
   full enough

to walk the block
   after all week

too cold
   outside to smile—

I think of you, warm
   in your underground room

reading the book
   of bone. It's hard going—

your body a dead
   language—

I've begun
   to feel, if not

hope then what
   comes just after—

or before—
   Let's not call it

regret, but
   this weight,

or weightlessness,
    or just

plain waiting.
    The ice wanting

again water.
    The streams of two planes

a cross fading.

I was so busy
    telling you this I forgot

to mention the sky—
    how in the dusk

its steely edges
    have just begun to rust.

I walk the line

The bags beneath
my eyes are packed

but won't leave—
neither can I—

My plane hit
by lightning.

So I check back into Vegas
feeling like late Elvis—

not broke but broken.
Hard to know

when you're sick
of this place, or just sick—

There's always roulette.

I only bet black.

Soon my money
gone like Johnny

Cash who left us
after a dozen almosts—

spinning the rigged wheel
like a tune.

In May, June went—then July,
August, & now Johnny

who we'll rename autumn after.
Sadder than

a wedding dress
in a thrift store—

Salvation's an army
& Sun the record

I once found Cash's face on
warped but still good

for 5 bucks.
Death does

a brisk business.
Checking out,

the next morning I thought
I saw God

playing the cheap slots, praying
he'll win

before he loses.

I give the wheel one last spin
playing the age

I'll soon be
if I'm lucky—

the age Jesus was
when his Daddy did him in—

& hit—

Dealer stacks chips & asks
Want to keep going?

My plane waiting
to fly me home again

I think hard a moment,
tip big, cash

out & split.

I hope it rains at my funeral

And fire. And sleet.
And cloud covering

Over everything.
And the cold.

Too soon—

And bargains
with the Devil later

You don't regret.

And begging.
And belief.

Why now Lord.

And snow sealing
shut your eyes.

Enough.

And pleading
with Death to dawdle.

An hour.
A fortune.

No matter how much—

And tomorrow
still the sun

Who quits for no one.

I dream a highway

GOD ranks second
at Mortal Kombat
behind WHY.

Regulars stay awhile
at the bar, asking
after Jim

who last year left
without a word—
& among the smoke I read Lorca

trying to remember
your face. Well drinks
half off. Too loud

to talk or
to not overhear
the barkeep's big plans

for Memorial Day.
I don't want to live
forever, just

a bit longer—but isn't that what
the first gods thought
learning they were immortal?

Tomorrow, & another,
& one day it dawns:
What if things keep on

like this? How long
is forever? *I watched*
the waitress for

a thousand years—
ask for a dollar
in change

to lose
in the machine—
or to tip whatever

sends you to the restroom
where the answers
aren't, but neither

are there questions—
just requests—*Don't
Look Down*

or *Thank God
For Drunk Girls.
Flush Twice*

*It's a Long Way
to Memphis.*
An unseen man

in the stall whistles
*Is That All
There Is?* Not even

a mirror to face—
just water, more machines
to keep your name

from passing on,
& someone's scrawled song
that could be ours:

*JD is still
dead & we
are still sad.*

I don't burn

Dear Darkness—consider this
my last attempt

to reach you. My previous
few missives

having boomeranged back
unread, postmarks blurred

by the gloved hands
that tried carrying

them to your door.
Or, torn

by the machines.
I wish

you could see the water
here, so clear

you can see the bottom—
though that's nothing

new for me. All afternoon
I let sun seep

my skin, steep me
like strong tea.

Despair,
if you've moved

I wish you would
send word

or ring.
How I would sing

like a kettle to keep you.

I am trying to break your heart

I am hoping
to hang your head

on my wall
in shame—

the slightest taxidermy
thrills me. Fish

forever leaping
on the living-room wall—

paperweights made
from the skulls

of small animals.
I want to wear

your smile on my sleeve
& break

your heart like a horse
or its leg. Weeks of being

bucked off, then
all at once, you're mine—

Put me down.

I want to call you *thine*

to tattoo *mercy*
along my knuckles. *I assassin*

down the avenue.
I hope

to have you forgotten
by noon. To know you

by your knees
palsied by prayer.

Loneliness is a science—

consider the taxidermist's
tender hands

trying to keep from losing
skin, the bobcat grin

of the living.

Cambridge Ode

Soon all will be gone,
the places I've known—
Elsie's, The Tasty, Tommy's Lunch,
replaced by lobster & *prix fixe* brunch.

Nothing's new about loss except everything
now is new—the cobbler one day disappears
like the very word *cobbler.*
My dry cleanser now does shoe repair.

One Potato Two Potato. That druggist
I never went to. Slowly every bookstore
shut down or moved—Star, McIntyre
& Moore—put out like lights. After 180 Years

We're Closing Our Doors. Even the Wursthaus—
where every visitor ate at first & cursed
for hours after, the place earning its name—
I miss avoiding, proving you were no more

a tourist. Ache & brick outlasts
even us—if lucky we leave not just a place
but a name. Soon, all gone: Tommy's,
The Tasty, Elsie's, me.

Dunk Tank

for Addie

This world is like the fair
in Cheboygan where

the Pageant Queen & her court
wander the midway, envied, bored—

where you try & try to hit
the tiny target

& even when you manage to, the clown
still won't go down—

instead, past the Veal Barn,
the bozo curses your slender arms

that want to stretch
all the way & push

him heckling down,
drowned,

in his watery cage.
You missed. Or maybe

we're the clown—our
faces fart,

makeup permanent
in a smile or frown, our feet

taunt the water, not
knowing when we'll fall—

Till then, let's fill

our stomachs with anything
fried, or served on sticks,

or better yet both—winning
at last the plush, stuffed elephant

our car barely fits.

Everybody Knows This Is Nowhere

I have driven for miles with bottles
left on my roof—

for miles folks pointing
out warnings

I thought welcomes.
I have waved back.

The sound
of broken glass

follows me around
like a stray.

Good boy.
Stay—

And the whales
washing themselves

ashore
nothing can save—

all day blankets wet
their skin like we're taught

to put fires out.

And the volunteers pushing them
back out at high tide

sleep well, exhausted, even
proud—before forty more,

the same, days later pilot
themselves ashore again,

blowholes opening
and closing like fists.

And the sound.

And the fires out west
started by someone

lighting love letters
she didn't want—

turns out to be a lie.

Blue blue windows
behind the stars.

And what if they had
been people instead

of whales, my mother wonders,
would that many

gather to save us?

Just enough
light to read.

Grievous Angel

Hope you know a lot more
than you're believing
                        —Gram Parsons

I used to believe more
than I knew—now

there's only the rain
I rely on, season

of monsoon moving
across the Plains.

Round here you can see
the storms arrive

from a ways away.

By the self-serve island
off the interstate

a lone seagull
wanders, walking

nowhere near water.
Who wants always

to be right?
Or alive?

Soon enough,
the sand

filling the mouth.
And—

I saw the light

We'll sweep out the ashes in the morning

—Gram Parsons

Just wing it—

doused in whisky, disguised
     as a funeral director

in flammable polyester,
     the hearse you hijack

will drag the stolen coffin
     to the desert, sparing the body

being flown home
     to Louisiana, there buried—

the deceased wanted
to be burned, someone overheard.

The ripening remains.

The reaping goes
     on without us

seeing—no longer do we bathe
     our own dead.

Busy yourself,
     being not yet buried—

The body you steal
     may well be your own—

In my hour of darkness

in my time of need,
light out for the desert

buy a six-pack, and gasoline
     enough to get you

there, enough to pour
      down the thirsty throat

of death—soaking the body
      beleaguered, bet against—

your garments rent.

Beg the light
to linger. The blaze you build

will shine the night
      like a shoe—

a thin wick
against the dark.

If heaven, if anything
      after, then

it too burns bright—
      for a time—

On Being the Only Black Person
at the Johnny Paycheck Concert

The man in the American flag
dress shirt wants to pick
a fight. He's been grabbing
women & high-

fiving his buddies all night.
We're here in Nashville
on our Meat Tour, getting the four
food groups in: chicken,

barbeque, cheeseburger, pork
chop sandwich still on the bone—
served with a pickle on a bun
and a half-full bottle of A.1.

The boot store also sells songs.
Johnny Cash's *Big River*
rolled out half-dozen times
along music row—requests

& tips—before we line up
like shots of Tennessee
sour-mash whisky
to see BR5-49, band named

for the telephone exchange
on the opening of *Hee Haw*.
Back when television
had no backup & you had to stand

to change channels, for an addict
kid like me Saturday-night TV
meant waiting out Lawrence Welk,
& then Buck Owens jumping out

of the corn, Minnie Pearl's hat
with the price tag still on it
dangling like a toe tag
on a dead man. The jokes

I never did get. Still the music told
what gingham would not—
heartbreak & history, voices
where accents are assets—

Close enough
for country music—
those twilight hours before *Love*
Boat became *Fantasy Island*

just as before the band who know
more Hank Williams than Hank
himself did, dead
in the back of his car

still headed toward a gig,
we must endure
coulda-beens like Johnny
Paycheck, who the poster

pictures young, handsome,
& pissed. His backup,
expanding-waist band
vamps till Johnny huffs,

washed up
neat & bearded, onstage,
the two steps to the risers
sending him out of breath.

Even jail, & years
of hard living,
don't deserve such
ashen fate. Paycheck

bounces along his set, enters
songs late & gets out
early, always ending with
Thank you all very much

no matter the thin applause.
Smoker's cough. Everyone
restless to hear his #1 pop
& country hit—*Take This Job*

and Shove It—
& while I hit the head

more out of boredom
than need, Paycheck obliges,
grudging into it, tonight less
an anthem against the Man

than a ditty disappointed
in itself—behind him the band
noodles solos while Paycheck,
spent, graduate

of anger management,
phones in
his resignation. Almost
an afterthought—

no encore—whoops
from the American flag
now too drunk to stand
or dance, in a town

that tonight, to Johnny, soon
dead, must seem
Cash Only—for now
Paycheck simply

smiles *Goodnight*—
wheezes—*You're too kind.*

Last Ditch Blues

Even Death
don't want me.

Spiders in my shoes.

Even God.

I tried
drinking strychnine

Or going to sleep
neath the railroad ties—

Always the light
found me first.

The Law.

Put me under arrest
for assaulting a freight—

Disturbing what peace.

(Turns out it
was only strych-eight.)

Tired of digging
my own grave.

Tired.

Spiders in my shoes.

The paperboy only
sold me bad news.

And wet at that.

The obit page said:
Not Today.

The weather blue too.

Stones all in my shoes.

Deep Six Blues

I overslept & was running
late for my own wake.

The professional mourners
who came

complained
they were underpaid.

What a eulogy
my enemies gave!

At least at last
I made the funny pages—

Man Survives

*Years Without
A Heart.*

Like me, the daisies
were on loan

from the old-folks home
& on their way

to being replaced
by plastic.

Thing is, I'm allergic

& even dead managed
to sneeze my way

through all the endless
off-key singing.

Eulogy

To allow silence
To admit it in us

always moving
Just past

senses, the darkness
What swallows us

and we live amongst
What lives amongst us

*

These grim anchors
That brief sanctity

the sea
Cast quite far

when you seek
—in your hats black

and kerchiefs—
to bury me

*

Do not weep
but once, and a long

time then
Thereafter eat till

your stomach spills over
No more! you'll cry

too full for your eyes
to leak

*

The words will wait

*

Place me in a plain
pine box I have been

for years building
It is splinters

not silver
It is filled of hair

*

Even the tongues
of bells shall still

*

You who will bear
my body along

Spirit me into the six
Do not startle

at its lack of weight
How light

Serenade

I wake to the cracked plate
of moon being thrown

across the room—
that'll fix me

for trying sleep.
Lately even night

has left me—
now even the machine

that makes the rain
has stopped sending

the sun away.
It is late,

or early, depending—

who's to say.
Who's to name

these ragged stars, this
light that waters

down the milky dark
before I down

it myself.
Sleep, I swear

there's no one else—
raise me up

in the near-night
& set me like

a tin toy to work,
clanking in the bare

broken bright.

YOUNG & SONS'
BAR-B-Q HEAVEN

Ode to Catfish

Old man,
despite your beard
& bald head
you still ain't old
enough to be dead—
you swim back
slipping through my hands
into the dark & I wake.
Even in dreams you are dead.
Your fresh, certain smell—
cornbread batter frying
in the pan—mornings still
fills my face
& I am glad. No matter
the pain it takes
to hold you, your barbs
& beard, you sustain me
& I wander
humming your hundred names—
brother, bullhead, paperskin, slick.
Remember the day, po boy,
you fried up catfish
with grits for breakfast, your mother
& sisters surrounding us
& you declared it
perfect? Sweet Jesus
you were right.
Fish hooks in my heart.
My plate full of bones
I'm scared to swallow.

Prayer for Black-Eyed Peas

Humbly, I come to you now
O bruised lord, beautiful
wounded legume,
in this time of plague, in my
very need. Ugly angel,
for years I have forsaken
you come New Year's Day,
have meant to meet you
where you live & not
managed to. I gave you up
like an unfaithful lover, but still
you nag me like a mother.
Like the brother I don't have
I need you now to confide in,
my eyes & yours darkened
by worry, my baby
shoes bronzed & lost.
Awkward antidote,
bring me luck & whatever
else you choose & I'll bend low
to shore you up. Part
of me misses you, part knows
you'll never leave, the rest
wants you to hear my every
unproud prayer. Wounded
God of the Ground, Our Lady
of Perpetual Toil & Dark Luck,
harbor me & I pledge each
inch of my waist not to waste
you, to clean my plate
each January & like you
not look back. You are
like the rice & gravy my Great
Aunt Toota cooked—you need,
& I with you, nothing else.
Holy sister, you are my father
planted along the road
one mile from where he

was born, brought full
circle, almost. You, the visitation
I pray for & what vision
I got—not quite
my father's second sight.
My grandmother saying
she dreams of me
& he every night. *Every*
night. Every night.
Small book of hours, quiet
captain, you are our future
born blind, eyes swole shut,
or sewn.

Ode to Gumbo

For weeks I have waited
for a day without death
or doubt. Instead
the sky set afire

or the flood
filling my face.
A stubborn drain
nothing can fix.

Every day death.
Every morning death
& every night
& evening

And each hour
a kind of winter—
all weather
is unkind. Too

hot, or cold
that creeps the bones.
Father, your face
a faith

I can no longer see.
Across the street
a dying, yet
still-standing tree.

*

So why not
make a soup
of what's left? Why
not boil & chop

something outside
the mind—let us
welcome winter
for a few hours, even

in summer. Some
say Gumbo
starts with *filé*
or with *roux,* begins

with flour & water
making sure
not to burn. I know Gumbo
starts with sorrow—

with hands that cannot wait
but must—with okra
& a slow boil
& things that cannot

be taught, like grace.
Done right,
Gumbo lasts for days.
Done right, it will feed

you & not let go.
Like grief
you can eat & eat
& still plenty

left. Food
of the saints,
Gumbo will outlast
even us—like pity,

you will curse it
& still hope
for the wing
of chicken bobbed

up from below.
Like God
Gumbo is hard
to get right

& I don't bother
asking for it outside
my mother's house.
Like life, there's no one

way to do it,
& a hundred ways,
from here to Sunday,
to get it dead wrong.

                *

Save all the songs.
I know none,
even this, that will
bring a father

back to his son.
Blood is thicker
than water under
any bridge

& Gumbo thicker
than that. It was
my father's mother
who taught mine how

to stir its dark mirror—
now it is me
who wishes to plumb
its secret

depths. Black
Angel, Madonna
of the Shadows,
Hail Mary strong

& dark as dirt,
Gumbo's scent fills
this house like silence
& tells me everything

has an afterlife, given
enough time & the right
touch. You need
okra, sausage, bones

of a bird, an entire
onion cut open
& wept over, stirring
cayenne in, till the end

burns the throat—
till we can amen
& pretend
such fiery

mercy is all we know.

Elegy for Maque Choux

Long before I had any clue
about grief, and worse,
when I thought
I knew—
             it was time
and the pain
of breathing—
             I sure
couldn't make maque choux.
Still, no one can do
it like my grandmother
could—sweet and spiced
at the same time,
                          in well
seasoned black pots that saw
more than their share
of fires, saw smoldering
woodstoves & firstborns lost
& now my father
                   placed under
the earth, & just
months later, a lifetime,
even my grandmother
gone.
          No more
maque choux.
                     No more gar
made to sing in a stew—
even tasting it I knew
no one else could lure
such a tune
out of bone.
                   I do not want
to get good
at grief—
             just to know again
that Indian corn
scraped clean, & tomato,

its sweet relief.
                    I know
now that grief is more
mirror, or terror,
than the slow hands
of time,
          my father's watch
that winds itself
only when on your wrist—
on the dresser, lost
in a drawer, it grows silent
& still, even the date
stops—
          as today, after
weeks of heat marooned
it from my arm
I put it back on
to find the date, for once,
correct—
                    marking the day after
my grandmother fell
& four months almost
to the day after my father
went into wherever
his watch does when no longer
in my hands—
                    its still
black face.

Ode to Sweet Potato Pie

Caramel. Coffee cake.
Chocolate I don't much love
anyway. Tough taffy.

Anything with nuts.
Or raisins. Goobers.
Even my Aunt Dixie's

apple pie recipe
or the sweet potato pie
my mother makes sing.

Even heaven. Even Boston
cream pie, Key Lime,
Baked Alaska, dense

flourless torte covered in raspberries
like a Bronx cheer.
Sherbet, spelt right,

and sandwiches
made of ice cream, even mint
or coffee I never drink,

even sherry, and smooth port
pulled up from shipwrecks
preserved on the bottom of the sea—

all this, & more, I would give up
to have you here, pumpkin-
colored father, cooking

for me—your hungry oven
humming—just one
more minute

Ode to Barbeque Sauce

In all the paintings of heaven
there is little

or no food—and an afterlife
minus okra

or barbeque or your arms
seems useless. Of course

it wasn't even heaven
you were after—

instead, as you once said,
I am trying to find

the perfect sauce—
Thing is, father, I'd say

you already had—the huge
bottle in your fridge I found

after the first
of your two funerals

held both honey
& sour, a manna none

but you could make
& I can only

hope to copy. Too busy
to write down & now

all our answers are maybes.
Tabasco, worcestershire, molasses,

Pickapeppa—nothing was right
for what all you wanted,

the sauce you sought
was like the farm

you bought & spent
hours on, trying to burn the fields

back to native grass—
at dusk killing

thistle, its purple
head everywhere alien.

Sounds like a life, alright—
trying to find what can't be

among the weeds, fighting
against time & the light

that, like that sauce
darkening your fallow fridge,

there never is
enough of.

Ode to Watermelon

Down here, in heaven,
there's little left

but waiting—in this
afterlife, this life

after your death,
there's always too much

sun, or never enough
shines. His shadow

scares the groundhog
indoors again. Lucky

for us, there's you,
watermelon—

small sun, long
lost kin, your grin

is what I miss
of this

bitter earth—your touch
turned toxic, to you

I've grown allergic—
your sweetness

stains my shirt
& chin less

& less. I've heard
that what you crave

about something is just
what later makes

its itch
choke your throat.

I know this world

is no welcome.
Only exit—

which is why, sweet
sister, your fire

fuels me cool.
Secret lover, tender

heart, I miss how
once—despite all guilt—

your dark
seeds' umpteen eyes

watched over me, grew
in me a tree.

Good Gourd, Georgia
ham, you are my cousin

born red—we thump
you like a drum

to learn how true
you are.

How sound.
Blood brother,

cut open you are a banner
red & seeded

with stars.
I want to devour

like grief, this life
to the rind—to leave

not white,
only green,

behind.

Ode to Turtle Soup

i.m. Leo Paul Pitre
d. 2005

How nice it must be not to be
alive—to wander

without worry
or not to wander

at all. To court sleep
no longer—

Here, the water
runs cold, & we dress

for yesterday. The distance
between premonition

& panic
is slim. Is your double

cousin, Leo Paul,
speaking at your funeral—

his father & your mother
were siblings, & vice versa—

how you told him last
you phoned, you'd seen

something horrible
in a dream, too horrible

to say.
         He shares
your middle name—

& I worry too your fate.
Death does not wait—

*

     Mudda saying *See*
that little boy?

pointing where there's none—
Hours later,

in that same spot,
right here, it's him

she'll join.
Not long

for this world.
        Not long
after, I'll speak to Leo

from his hospital room, recovering,
routine, laughing,

hours before the threes
come & get him—dead

by dawn—brought back down
to that same, too soft,

Louisiana ground.
Lay me like

a burden down.

     *

This life leaves us
breathless
  & begging—

This world is
no welcome.

The world is a turtle
weighting
   your back—

   Let us not
   forget solace—

Let us make
of it a meal
     like my grandmother would

of food we cannot stand, just
because someone we love

craves it. Turtle
soup. Mudfish.
        Help yourself

my grandmother would say—
would tell you in a hot minute

I never served no body
& won't start now.

Never did see her
ever eat
    sitting down.

      *

The race
   is long.

      *

Our Lady
of Eve's Hunger,
    Mudda—

I come now
with my plate
   again empty

I come with arms full
of pleas, terrapin-slow

& steady, hoping
your cast iron will feed me—

to savor the song
of gravel road,

of bayou & valley—
          the widow's moan—

what boils down
   our bones.

Song of Cracklin

Little heaven,
marked man,

I've seen you turn
a bag see-through

Then escape—
Homemade Houdini

God of grease
& heartburn

You test me
& my nerve.

Salt-junkie,
you're Russian

Roulette—
delicious as death—

God of grief
& heartattack

Hourglass we hope
to outlast

How you clog
the house with talk

& laughter for days,
the black skillet singing

Your name.

Ode to Hot Sauce

Your leaving tastes
of nothing. Numb,

I reach for you
to cover my tongue

like the burnt word
of God—surrender

all to you, my fiery
sacrifice. My father

never admitted anything
was too hot

for him, even as the sweat
drained down his forehead,

found his worn collar
& eyes. You make mine

water & even water
won't quench you.

Only bread bests you.
Only the earth cools

& quiets this leftover
life, lights

my open mouth.
These days I taste

only its roof—
my house

on fire, all the doors
locked, windows latched

like my heart. My heart.
Carve it out

& on the pyre—
after the witch hunt

& the devil's
trial, after repentance

& the bright
blaze of belief—

it will outlive even
the final flame.

This is why I take
your sweet sting

into my eyes
& mouth like turpentine, rise

& try to face
the furnace of the day.

Ode to Pepper Vinegar

You sat in the tomb

of our family fridge
for years, without

fail. You were all

I wanted covering
my greens, satisfaction

I've since sought

for years in restaurants
which claimed soul, but neither

knew you nor

your vinegar prayer.
Baby brother

of bitterness, soothsayer,

you taught
me the difference between loss

& holding on. Next to the neon

of the maraschino cherries,
you floated & stayed

constant as a flame

on an unknown soldier's grave—
I never did know

how you got here

you just were. Adrift
in your mason jar

you were a briny bit of where

we came from, rusty lid
awaiting our touch

& tongue—you were faith

in the everyday, not rare
as the sugarcane

my grandparents sent north

come Christmas, drained
sweet & dry, delicious, gone

by New Year's—

no, you were nearer,
familiar, the thump

thump of an upright bass

or the brass
of a funeral band

bringing us home.

Ode to Fig Preserves

First fruit,
fig that Eve
plucked & sent us
here, hereafter, in need
of need, you bowed the tree
behind my grandparents' house—
forbidden food for the cows
who came & grazed
at the treelimbs leaned
heavy over the fence. Nothing
scared them away.
My grandfather's *git*
or whistle or whip
he'd braided himself
proved useless—the fruit
too delicious for the spotted
moaning ruminants to resist.
Picked, split apart
like small, pink, pip-
filled hearts, knowledge
we no longer want, figs
sweet enough to eat straight
from the tree, or saved
& carried north
in our exile, preserved
for winter's long embrace
& spread shiny
on biscuits each Sunday.
Salvation's imperfect
potion, & portion. Only
my father & his shotgun
could shoo them cows
stubborn as ghosts
from behind the house—
come see, & me holding
the butt tight against
my shoulder, the barrel
cradled in my arms like a father

found dead in a field, *you better hold on*
or you'll break your shoulder—
now squeeze—& instead
it is the silence
we shatter, the cows
who skedaddle, tack
around slow—buckshot
catapulting above fields
I now own, falling where
I don't know, scattered
like seeds I gather
now bloom into stone.

Ode to Cushaw

i.m. Sherman Newton
d. 2007

          Beneath the green
of our August garden overgrown
since I'd returned
from my summer spent cousined
out west—
                    flown solo,
six, I was met by the City
of Angels as I fear
heaven might—me last
off the flight, escorted by the lady
in blue down the gangplank,
wings pinned
to my shoulders & no one
claims me—
                    only I, half-pint, returned,
could unearth what might be, worming
my way beneath. Like God
I found you, giant gourd, drug
you like a shadow behind me,
swimming toward the light.
          Poor man's pumpkin,
prodigal son, thin-skinned kin
to melon & me, you are among us
unknown, like my mother's father
she rarely knew, I barely—
                    that's him standing
at the altar of Springfield Baptist,
silent deacon awaiting any sinners,
amen, & my grown mother crying
through the hymns—that's him,
amen, his mind now weedy, now
gone, amen, buried yesterday,
my mother's eyes dry.
          Cushaw, mystery
man, I thought you an accident,
just erupted here, immaculate—
                    size of almost ten months

in the womb, green & white, belly large
as a tombstone in the photo
of me grinning with you, gentle
giant, the snapshot sent
to my grandmother who, turns out,
gave us the seed you once slept in—
awoken now, it is she who calls you
cushaw & teaches us how
to fix you.
                    Scrape
the insides clean & cook,
stirring, butter, brown sugar,
then serve like sweet potatoes
though more sour.
          So this
is what the past
tastes like—
                    like promise,
or promises, something
unspoken & never seen
again, but known
by heart.
          The first flinch
            of the Polaroid's flash—
All our bright vanishings—
                    If ever
you need someone to vouch
for you, Cushaw, just ask—
    I will give you my name,
love child, my heirloom gourd
& Wednesday's child—god of what
doesn't spoil—Saviour
of all the small,
unclaimed things
of this world.

Ode to Boudin

You are the chewing gum
of God. You are the reason
I know that skin
is only that, holds
more than it meets.
The heart of you is something
I don't quite get
but don't want to. Even
a fool like me can see
your broken
beauty, the way
out in this world where most
things disappear, driven
into ground, you are ground
already, & like rice
you rise. Drunken deacon,
sausage's half-brother,
jambalaya's baby mama,
you bring me back
to the beginning, to where things live
again. Homemade saviour,
you fed me the day
my father sat under flowers
white as the gloves of pallbearers
tossed on his bier.
Soon, hands will lower him
into ground richer
than even you.
For now, root of all
remembrance, your thick chain
sets me spinning, thinking
of how, like the small,
perfect, possible, silent soul
you spill out
like music, my daddy
dead, or grief,
or both—afterward his sisters

my aunts dancing
in the yard to a car radio
tuned to zydeco
beneath the pecan trees.

Acknowledgments

Poems in this volume appeared in the following
journals, often in earlier versions:

Boston Review: "Everybody Knows This Is Nowhere"

Callaloo: "Nineteen Seventy-Five"; "Sweet Blood"

Harvard Review: "I hope it rains at my funeral"; "Last Ditch Blues"

Jubilat: "I saw the light"

Kenyon Review: "Tuff Buddies"; "No Offense"; "Casting"; "I shall be released"; "Grievous Angel"; "Ode to Gumbo"

Meatpaper: "Ode to Boudin"

New England Review: "Book Rate"

New Letters: "Another Autumn Elegy"; "I dream a highway"; "Ode to Catfish"; "Ode to Pepper Vinegar"; "Uncles (Play)"

The New Yorker: "Serenade"; "Farm Team"; "Slow Drag Blues"

Oxford American: "Ode to Chicken"; "Ode to Kitchen Grease"; "I walk the line"; "See That My Grave Is Kept Clean"; "Something Borrowed Blues"

Poetry: "Bling Bling Blues"; "Ode to the Midwest"

Poetry Northwest: "On Being Blind"; "Hang Dog Blues"; "I am trying to break your heart"

Ploughshares: "Ode to Greens"

The Progressive: "Flash Flood Blues"

A Public Space: "I don't burn"

Tin House: "Ring of Fire"; "May Day Blues"; "Lime Light Blues"

Virginia Quarterly Review: "Watching the Good Trains Go By"; "Hard Headed Blues"; "Say When"; "Lullaby"; "Black Cat Blues"; "Dirty Deal Blues"; "Quartet"

"Black Cat Blues" was reprinted in *Best American Poetry 2005.* "Casting" was reprinted in Clarence Major's anthology *The Garden Thrives.* "Hard Headed Blues" was reprinted in the Cave Canem poetry anthology, *Gathering Ground.* "Ode to Greens" was issued in a limited-edition broadside designed by Slaughter Group and printed at Kempis Press in collaboration with the UAB Writers' Series. "Ode to Pork first appeared as a broadside celebrating the Tenth Southern Foodways Symposium in fall 2007.

The italics in "Ring of Fire" are quotes from friends. The first set of italicized lines in "I dream a highway" are from a song of that title by Gillian Welch; the title "I am trying to break your heart" and the poem's italics are from a Wilco song; "Everybody Knows This is Nowhere" is a Neil Young song, though the italics are taken from his "Helpless."

Thanks to the Guggenheim and NEA Literature Fellowships that allowed me to complete this book. And to Mack: welcome.

A Note About the Author

Kevin Young is the author of five previous collections of poetry and the editor of the Library of America's *John Berryman: Selected Poems*, the Everyman's Library Pocket Poets anthologies *Blue Poems* and *Jazz Poems*, and *Giant Steps: The New Generation of African American Writers*. His book *Jelly Roll* was a finalist for the National Book Award and the Los Angeles Times Book Prize, and won the Paterson Poetry Prize. His collection *For the Confederate Dead* won the 2007 Quill Award for poetry and the Paterson Award for Sustained Literary Achievement. *Dear Darkness* won the Southern Independent Bookseller Award and the Julia Ward Howe Prize. The recipient of a Guggenheim Fellowship, Young is currently the Atticus Haygood Professor of English and Creative Writing and curator of Literary Collections at the Raymond Danowski Poetry Library at Emory University in Atlanta.

www.kevinyoungpoetry.com

A Note on the Type

*This book was set in Granjon, a type named for
Robert Granjon, a type cutter and printer active in
Europe from 1523 to 1590. However, it more
closely resembles a type used by Claude Garamond
(ca. 1480–1561) in his beautiful French books
than any of Granjon's types.*

*Composed by Creative Graphics, Allentown,
Pennsylvania
Printed and bound by Thomson-Shore,
Dexter, Michigan
Designed by Anthea Lingeman*